HOW DOES
IT GROW?

DANDELION

Jinny Johnson

Illustrations by Graham Rosewarne

FRANKLIN WATTS
LONDON•SYDNEY

An Appleseed Editions book

First published in 2009 by Franklin Watts
338 Euston Road, London NW1 3BH

Franklin Watts Australia
Hachette Children's Books
Level 17/207 Kent St, Sydney, NSW 2000

Created by Appleseed Editions Ltd,
Well House, Friars Hill, Guestling,
East Sussex TN35 4ET

Designed by Helen James
Edited by Mary-Jane Wilkins
Picture research by Su Alexander

ISBN 978 0 7496 8790 8

Dewey Classification: 583'.99

A CIP catalogue for this book is available from the British Library.

Photograph acknowledgements
page 5 Terry Why/Photolibrary Group; 19 Bruce Wellman/Photolibrary Group;
25 Mark Newman/Photolibrary Group; 28 JTB Photo/Photolibrary Group
Front cover Bruce Wellman/Photolibrary Group

Printed in China

Franklin Watts is a division of Hachette Children's Books,
an Hachette UK company.
www.hachette.co.uk

Contents

Carried by the wind

A **dandelion** plant starts life as a **seed-like fruit**, smaller than a grain of rice. Each tiny fruit contains a **single seed**.

A dandelion seed has a long stalk. This has some **fluffy threads** on top, which act like a **parachute**.

The seed is carried off by the **wind** and may land **far away** from the parent plant.

DANDELION SEEDS ARE
CARRIED AWAY BY THE WIND.

What happens to the seed?

New leaves

Soon **bigger leaves** appear.
They have **jagged edges**
which look like teeth.

The dandelion's name might
come from its French name,
dents de lion, which means
lion's teeth.

Dandelion leaves grow **close
together** near the **ground**.

Do you think
these leaves look
like lion's teeth?

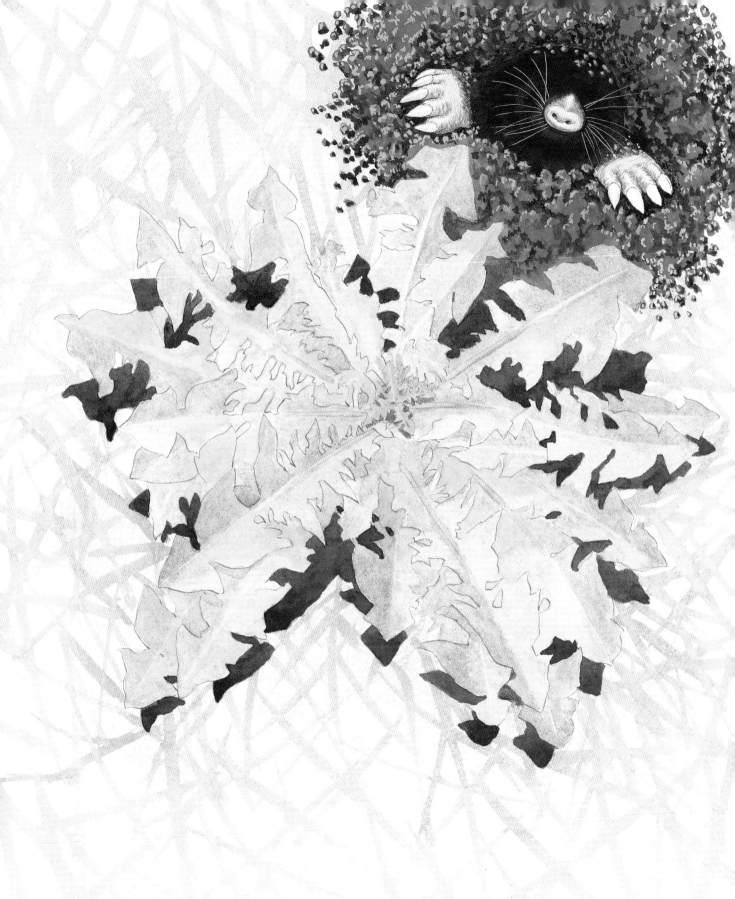

What does the dandelion need to help it grow?

Making food

Like all **plants**, dandelions
need **water** and **sunlight**
to help them grow.

Plants make their own food.
The **green leaves** use **water**,
sunlight and a **gas** called
carbon dioxide in the air
to **make** their **food**.

MOST DANDELION LEAVES
ARE ABOUT 20 CM LONG,
BUT SOME GROW BIGGER.

10

When do the flowers grow?

Stems and buds

Once the plant has lots of **leaves** several **stems** grow up from the centre of the plant.

The stems are **straight** and **hollow**. If a stem breaks, **sticky sap** oozes out.

A **flower bud** grows at the top of the stem. Around the bud there are a special kind of **green leaves** called **bracts**.

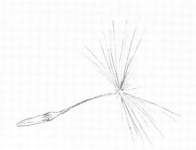

THE BRACTS AROUND THE BUD HELP TO PROTECT IT FROM INSECTS.

What does the bud open into?

Dandelion flowers

The **bud** opens into a beautiful **yellow** dandelion flower.

In fact a dandelion isn't a single flower. It is **100** or more **tiny flowers** that grow tightly together. The tiny flowers are called **florets**.

Each floret is **long** and **thin** and has **five little teeth** at the top.

Does the flower stay open all the time?

Open and closed

The dandelion flower **opens** in the **morning** when the sun rises.

Towards the end of the **afternoon** it **closes** up again for the night, with the green leaves tight around it.

The dandelion often **closes** when **rain is coming**, too. So you can look at a dandelion to find out whether you need to wear a **raincoat**.

Do insects like dandelion flowers?

Insects and dandelions

Insects love dandelion flowers.
Bees, **butterflies** and **hoverflies**
visit the yellow flowers to **feed** on
the **nectar** and **pollen**.

The flower has both **male and
female** parts. The dandelion
plant can make **seeds** on its own,
without any help from insects.

Dandelion plants start flowering
early in the year and keep
flowering all through the **summer**.
This makes them **useful plants
for bees**.

A HONEYBEE ON A
DANDELION FLOWER.
LOOK AT ALL THE YELLOW
POLLEN ON ITS BACK LEG.

What eats dandelions?

Tasty leaves?

Many other creatures like dandelions. **Rabbits and mice** nibble the leaves and birds love **to eat the seeds**.

Goats and **pigs** gobble up whole **dandelions**, but sheep, cows and horses don't seem to enjoy them. They may not like the **bitter taste** of the leaves.

RABBITS LIKE TO EAT DANDELION FLOWERS AS WELL AS THE LEAVES.

What happens to the flowers?

Seed ball

After a **week or two** the bright yellow flower **starts to fade**. The individual florets that make up the flower head fall.

The leaves close up around the **dying flower** and it looks almost like a bud again. Inside, the **seeds** are **developing**.

Slowly the **flower head** turns into a **seed ball**.

What is the seed ball?

Dandelion clock

The **seed ball** is a **mass** of dandelion **seeds**. Every seed has a stalk tipped with a **parachute** of fluffy **threads**.

The seed ball is often called a **dandelion clock**. You've probably **blown** on a dandelion seed ball and **counted how many** times you have to blow before all the **seeds** are gone.

LOTS OF
DANDELION
CLOCKS JUST
WAITING FOR
A PUFF OF WIND.

What happens to the seeds?

Starting again

The wind **blows away** the **seeds**. As the seed ball forms, the **stem grows longer** so it stands above the leaves to catch the **breeze**.

With every **gust of wind**, more seeds blow away on their **parachutes**. Every seed has tiny **spines** which point backwards. These help the seeds stay in the **soil** when they land so they can grow into **new plants**.

Words to remember

bract

A kind of thick leaf that grows around a flower bud.

bud

A part of a plant that will grow into a leaf or flower.

carbon dioxide

A gas in the air that plants use to make food.

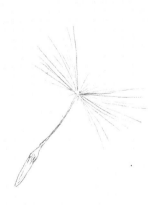

floret

One small flower in a group of flowers.

fruit

The part of a plant that contains its seeds.

nectar

A sugary liquid in flowers.

pollen

Tiny powdery grains made by flowers.

sap

Sticky liquid inside plant stems.

seed

A seed is the part of a plant from which new plants can grow. A seed ball is a group of seeds.

shoot

New growth on a plant.

Websites

Dandelion watch
http://www.naturewatch.ca/english/plantwatch/dandelion/

Arkive
http://www.arkive.org/common-dandelion/taraxacum-officinale-agg/

Science TV
http://www.science.tv/watch/136124592c8d4825a06f/
Dandelion-(Taraxacum)-Opening-Timelapse

Index